KB276132

Alien Adventure

About Wise & Wide

- A systematic 6-level English reading program based on Lexile® measures
- Diverse and interesting topics chosen from the elementary curriculums of Korea and English speaking western countries
- Well-written books in various forms including fiction stories, descriptive texts, and classics retold
- The informative but original fiction stories grab your interest, leading to the easy and clear understanding of the educational content.
- Improve thinking skills with solid after-reading activities at all levels of the series.

Wise & Wide is a 6-level English reading program that consists of 60 books and each level is systematically divided by Lexile® measures. The Lexile® Framework for Reading is the most popular reading measuring system in American formal education curriculums and many English programs. Over 20 out of 50 states in the U.S. mark Lexile® measures directly on students' final report cards and over 300 well-known publishers adopt and use Lexile® measures.

Experience many kinds of readings written by professional writers from the U.S. and England. They used interesting topics that were carefully chosen after analyzing elementary curriculums from around the world including Korea, the U.S., England, and Australia among many others. Comprehensive after-reading activities including graphic organizers, speaking tasks, and After-reading Tests are ready for you.

Levels in the series and their corresponding Lexile® measures

Level	Lexile® measures	U.S. Grade
Level 1	Below 200L	Pre K - K
Level 2	190L - 400L	Lower Grade 1
Level 3	350L - 530L	Upper Grade 1
Level 4	420L - 650L	Grade 2
Level 5	520L - 940L	Grade 3 - 4
Level 6	830L - 1070L	Grade 5 - 6

* Smart Readers: Wise & Wide level 1 is applicable to the preschool level in the U.S.

* The source of the relationship between Lexile® measures and U.S. school grades: CCSS(Common Core State Standards) FOR ENGLISH LANGUAGE ARTS, APPENDIX A (2012, which is used by 45 states in the U.S.)

Topic List

	Level 1	Level 2	Level 3	Level 4	Level 5	Level 6
Book 1	Science>Biology: The hibernation of animals Story	Science>Biology: Living and nonliving things Story	Science>Biology> Animals & the Environment: Sea otters Story	Environment> Living with nature: The diver & the persimmon tree Story	Science>Biology> Animal: Amazing animals of the Amazon Story	Science>Biology: Germs, transmitted diseases Story
Book 2	Literature> World classics: Aesop's fables Story	Literature> Traditional fairy tale: Old tales about stones Story	Social Studies> Economy: To run a business to make and save money Story	Science>Biology> Plants: Photosynthesis Story	Science>Earth science: Earth's layers, earthquakes, volcanoes, and earth's atmosphere Report	Mathematics> Sequence: The golden ratio & the Fibonacci sequence Story
Book 3	Science>Physics: How shadows are formed Story	Literature> World classics: Peter Pan Story	Science>Scientific technology: Nanobots Story	Literature>Myths: World's creation stories Story	Literature> Legend: The story of King Arthur Story	Literature>Myths: Constellation myths Story
Book 4	Literature> Traditional literature: The Talmud Story	Science>Biology> Animal: Polar bears Story	Science>Biology> Animal: Mountain gorillas Story	Social Studies> Cultural anthropology: Amazing ancient cultures of the world Story	Science> Earth science: Clouds and weather Story	Literature> Human & animals: The friendship between a girl and a horse Story
Book 5	Social Studies> Ethics: Rules in daily life Story	Science>Biology: The five senses Report	Social Studies> Cultural anthropology: Astonishing festivals Report	Art>Music: Stories from two operas Story	Social Studies> World culture & history: The Renaissance Story	Sports> Board sports: Surfing & snowboarding Story
Book 6	Social Studies> World geography & travel: Tourist attractions around the world Story	Science>Biology> Animal: Dinosaurs Story	Science> Astronomy: The solar system Story	Social Studies> People: Three great people who overcame hardships Story	Science>Scientific technology: The wonderful world of robots Report	Art>Music: Composers of the Romantic Era Report
Book 7	Science> Space science: The life of astronauts Report	Social Studies> Cultural anthropology: Mythological monsters from around the world Report	Mathematics> Elementary mathematics: Numbers, measurement, shapes and data Report	Science & Social Studies> Technology & culture: Inventions from around the world Report	Art>Works of art: Famous paintings Report	Social Studies> Human & animals: Animals in action for human Report
Book 8	Social Studies> Cultural anthropology: Various living cultures of the world Story	Art>Music: Instruments in the orchestra Story	Social Studies> Life safety: Learning and using outdoor survival skills Story	Social Studies> History: The California Gold Rush Report	Social Studies & Science> Psychology: Psychology in everyday life Story	Literature> World classics: The Merchant of Venice Story
Book 9	Social Studies> Jobs: Interviews about jobs Report	Science>Scientific technology: Developments in technology in different times Story	Social Studies> Politics>Election: Running for 3rd grade class president Story	Literature> World classics: Stories of Sherlock Holmes Story	Literature> World classics: Adrift in the Pacific Story	Social Studies> History & People: Great world leaders in history Report
Book 10	Literature>Traditional fairy tale: Eastern and Western folk tales on the same theme Story	Sports>Winter sports: Various aspects of some Winter Olympic sports Report	Literature> World classics: Short stories by O. Henry Story	Sports> Ball games: Various aspects of popular ball games Report	Social Studies> History: Famous events that changed world history Report	Art & Social Studies> Art: Stories about the creation, distribution, and preservation of paintings Report

How to Use This Book

•Before Reading

You can easily find the topic and what kind of story you are about to read.

•The text

All the stories were written by professional writers from the U.S. and England, so you will read authentic and appropriate English sentences and expressions in every book in the series.

•Pop Quiz

Check out right away if you understand what you have just read by solving a pop quiz that checks your comprehension.

•Key Words

The key words and expressions on each page are listed for you to easily study them.

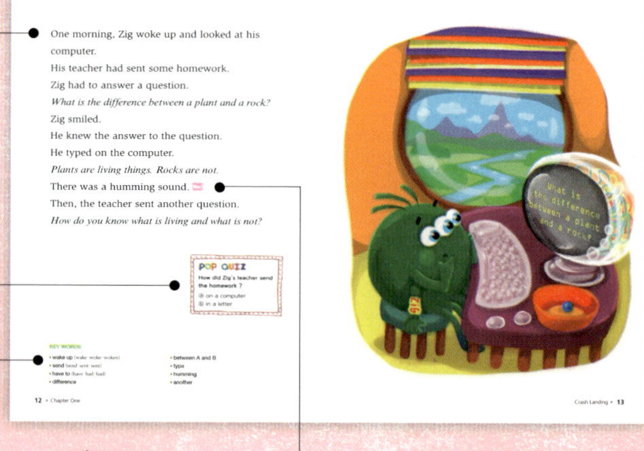

•Aha! Tips

Download free Korean explanations at *www.ihappyhouse.co.kr* for all of the sentences marked with "Aha!". These explain cultural, scientific, and economic knowledge or they deal with aspects of English such as grammatical structures or idiomatic expressions. There are lots of "Aha! Tips" to help you understand the text.

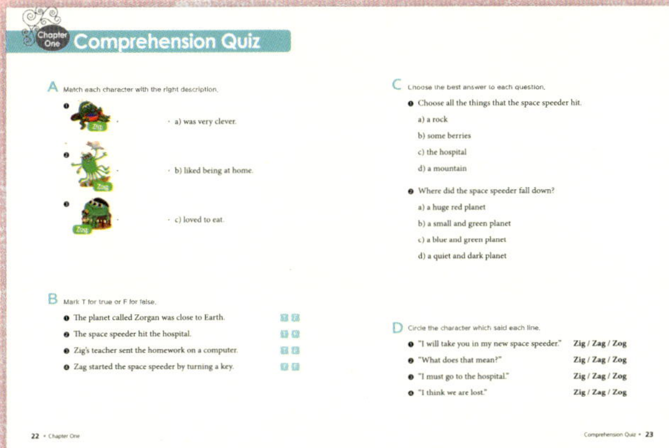

•Comprehension Quiz

After reading one chapter, solve various questions to find out if you fully understand the content.

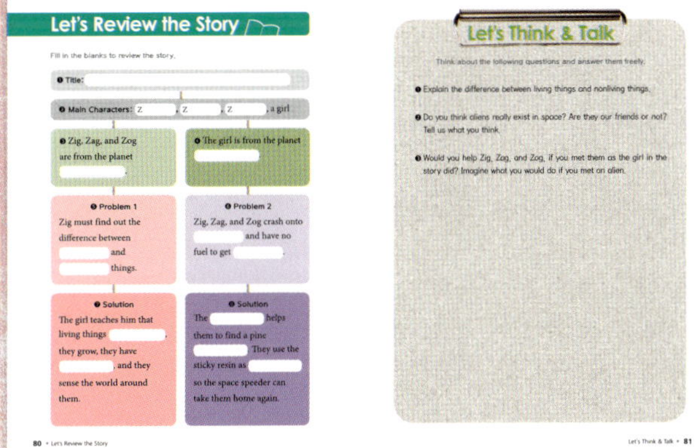

•Let's Review the Story /
•Let's Think & Talk

Fill in the blanks in the organizer to summarize the whole story. Express your own thinking and feelings about the story by answering the questions. You can build up logic and reasoning skills for your essay examinations in the future.

Appendix

Audio CD

In the CD audio book form, the texts are read vividly by American professional voice actors.

After-reading Test

Solve an additionally provided After-reading Test for each book.

The Korean translation, Answer Keys, a Word Quiz, a Word List, and Aha! Tips for each book

You can download them for free at *www.ihappyhouse.co.kr*

Before Reading

Alien Adventure

Level 2-1,
Lexile® 240L

•Science〉Biology
•Story

Living and nonliving things?

Have you ever heard of 'Living things' and 'Nonliving things'? Living things are live while nonliving things aren't. We usually call humans and animals living things. We usually call things that we use – phones, computers, etc. – nonliving things.

In the book, aliens make a forced landing on Earth. Through their adventure, we will find out what living things and nonliving things are and the differences between them. Before reading the book, look at the pictures below first. Then, mark the living things and the nonliving things appropriately and tell us why you grouped them that way.

Summary

A green face and body, four arms and seven legs! Is it a monster? No. It is a cute green alien and his friends. They are Zig, Zag and Zog, who live in a far-away planet called Zorgan. One day, Zig's feet turned blue, so Zag and Zog got on Zag's space speeder to take him to the hospital. But unfortunately, the three alien friends had to make a forced landing on Earth instead of going to the alien hospital. They were out of fuel and the computer in the space speeder was broken, so they had to find alternative fuel on earth. They came out of the speeder and met a girl. With her help, the three alien friends tried to get back home…

Will they be able to go back home safely?

Contents

Alien Adventure

2 About Wise & Wide

4 How to Use This Book

6 Before Reading

Chapter One
10 Crash Landing
22 Comprehension Quiz

Chapter Two
24 The Aliens from Earth
42 Comprehension Quiz

Chapter Three
44 A Hiding Game
62 Comprehension Quiz

Chapter Four
64 Sticky Stuff
78 Comprehension Quiz

80 Let's Review the Story

81 Let's Think & Talk

82 Let's Review the Story (Answers)

83 After-reading Test

Alien Adventure

Crash Landing

Zig, Zag, and Zog lived on a cool, green planet.

It was a bit like Earth.

But it was a long way out in space.

The planet was called Zorgan. 

Zig loved to eat.

Most of all, he loved blue berries.

Zag was very clever.

He could drive a space speeder.

Zog just liked to be with his friends.

He loved his home most of all.

▲ planet (Jupiter)

One morning, Zig woke up and looked at his computer.

His teacher had sent some homework.

Zig had to answer a question.

What is the difference between a plant and a rock?

Zig smiled.

He knew the answer to the question.

He typed on the computer.

Plants are living things. Rocks are not.

There was a humming sound. **Aha!**

Then, the teacher sent another question.

How do you know what is living and what is not?

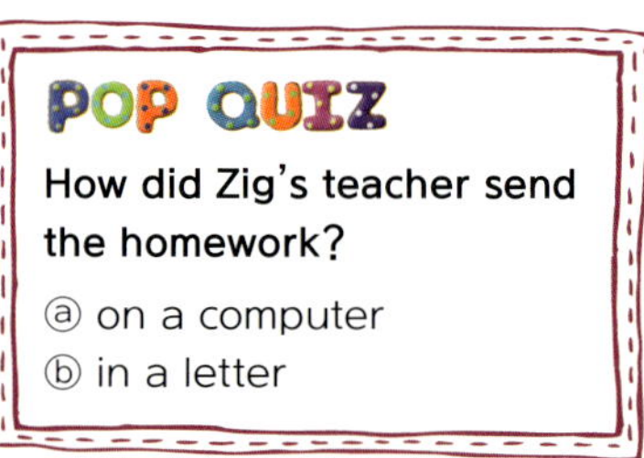

KEY WORDS

- **wake up** (wake-woke-woken)
- **send** (send-sent-sent)
- **have to** (have-had-had)
- **difference**

- **between A and B**
- **type**
- **humming**
- **another**

What is
the difference
between a plant
and a rock?

Zig thought hard.

"Aha!" he said.

"Perhaps all soft things are living things."

But he looked at his fluffy blanket.

It was not a living thing.

Zig did not know the answer to the question.

He needed to find out.

KEY WORDS

- **think** (think-thought-thought)
- **perhaps**
- **fluffy**
- blanket
- need to + *Verb*
- find out

Zig looked at his feet.

Something was wrong.

They were not green anymore.

They were blue!

He jumped up.

He ate some blue berries.

He ran to find Zag and Zog.

"Help me!" he said.

"I must go to the hospital."

"I will take you," said Zag.

"I will take you in my new space speeder.

It goes very fast."

So Zag and Zog helped Zig into the space speeder.

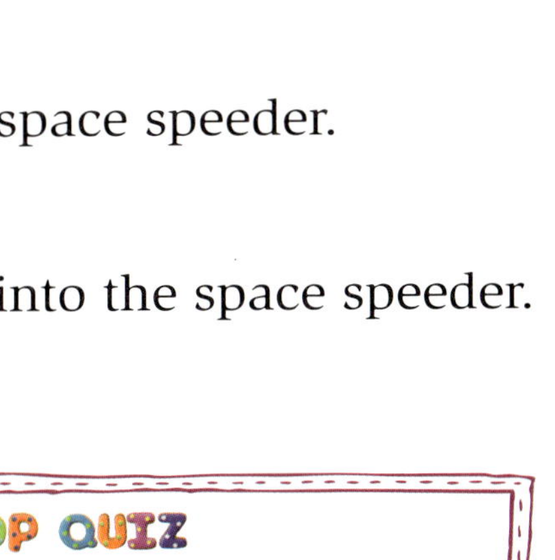

POP QUIZ

Why did Zig want to go to the hospital?

ⓐ He felt sick.
ⓑ His feet had changed color.

KEY WORDS

- wrong
- not ~ anymore
- jump up

- must (= have to)
- take (take-took-taken)
- help into

Zag pressed a switch.

The engine began to hum.

The space speeder shot up into the sky.

Then, it fell back down again.

CRASH!

The space speeder hit a rock.

BASH!

It bumped into the side of a mountain.

Zag pressed another switch.

- engine
- begin (begin-began-begun)
- hum
- shoot up (shoot-shot-shot)
- fall back down (fall-fell-fallen)
- crash
- bash
- bump

The space speeder shot up into the sky again.

Higher and higher it went. **Aha!**

The sky grew darker.

The jungle was far below.

All the plants looked tiny.

"Where are we going?" cried Zig.

"This is not the way to the hospital."

"Something is wrong," said Zag.

"I pressed the wrong switch."

The stars grew brighter.

They were out in space.

"I think we are lost," said Zag.

Zog began to cry.

"Turn around," he said.

"I do not know how," said Zag.

"This is a new space speeder.

The switches are not the same as my old one."

On and on they flew.

They saw blue planets and red ones.

There were huge planets and tiny ones.

"Something is wrong," said Zag.

"We do not have much fuel left."

Zig and Zog looked at each other.

"What does that mean?" they said.

"If we run out of fuel, the space speeder will…"

began Zag. Aha!

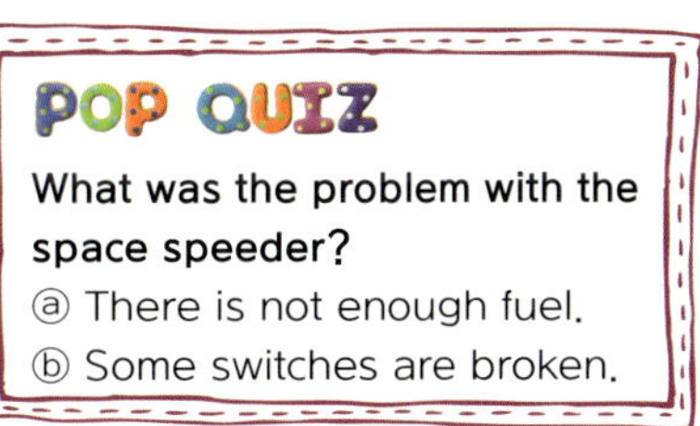

KEY WORDS

- be lost
- turn around
- the same as
- on and on
- tiny
- fuel
- each other
- if
- run out of

The engine stopped humming.

There was no sound at all.

"The space speeder will... what?" asked Zog.

Suddenly, the space speeder began to fall.

Down and down it went.

It fell toward a blue and green planet.

"My head and arms are turning blue!" said Zig.

"Hold on tight," said Zag.

"We are going to crash." Aha!

Zig shut his eyes.

Zog held his breath.

Zag pressed lots of switches.

Still, the space speeder fell.

There was a big BUMP.

There was a big BANG.

All the lights went off.

Everything was still.

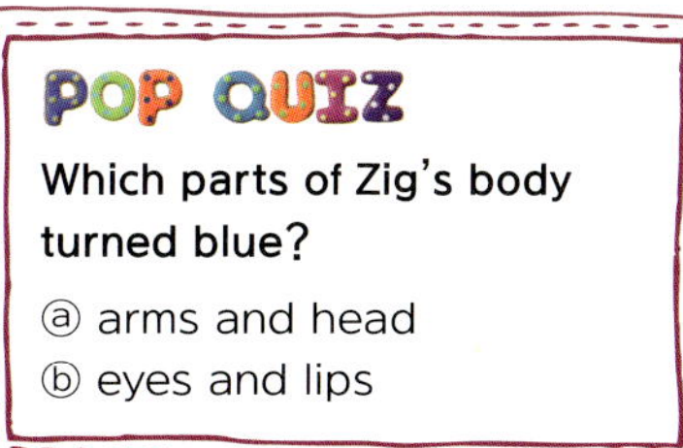

POP QUIZ

Which parts of Zig's body turned blue?

ⓐ arms and head
ⓑ eyes and lips

KEY WORDS

- suddenly
- toward
- hold on tight
  (hold-held-held)
- shut (shut-shut-shut)
- hold one's breath
- still
- bump
- bang
- go off (go-went-gone)

Comprehension Quiz

A   Match each character with the right description.

Zig

Zag

Zog

- a) was very clever.
- b) liked being at home.
- c) loved to eat.

B   Mark T for true or F for false.

1. The planet called Zorgan was close to Earth.   T   F
2. The space speeder hit the hospital.   T   F
3. Zig's teacher sent the homework on a computer.   T   F
4. Zag started the space speeder by turning a key.   T   F

C Choose the best answer to each question.

❶ Choose all the things that the space speeder hit.

a) a rock

b) some berries

c) the hospital

d) a mountain

❷ Where did the space speeder fall down?

a) a huge red planet

b) a small and green planet

c) a blue and green planet

d) a quiet and dark planet

D Circle the character which said each line.

❶ "I will take you in my new space speeder."   **Zig / Zag / Zog**

❷ "What does that mean?"   **Zig / Zag / Zog**

❸ "I must go to the hospital."   **Zig / Zag / Zog**

❹ "I think we are lost."   **Zig / Zag / Zog**

The Aliens from Earth

Zig opened all three of his eyes.

He wiggled all four of his arms.

They were still blue.

But they did not hurt.

"Is everyone all right?" he said.

"At least we are still alive," groaned Zag.

He rubbed his head.

"But where are we?" asked Zog.

Zag looked at the computer.

The screen was blank.

He pressed a button.

A pale green light glowed.

"Welcome to the planet called Earth," said a
voice.

It came from inside the computer.

"Earth?" said Zog.

"I have never heard of it." **Aha!**

"You have no fuel left," said the computer.

"Find more fuel at once."

"What kind of fuel do we need?" asked Zag.

The computer made a fizzing sound.

Smoke came out of it.

"Find a pine tree," said the computer.

"Use the resin. It is like Zorgan fuel."

Zog frowned.

"What is a pine tree?" he said.

"What is resin?"

"A pine tree is a living thing."

The computer crackled.

"Resin is the sticky stuff inside."

There was a loud bang.

The light on the screen went off.

There was a horrid burning smell.

▲ resin

KEY WORDS

▪ fizzing	▪ frown	▪ stuff	▪ burning
▪ pine tree	▪ crackle	▪ loud	▪ broken
▪ resin	▪ sticky	▪ horrid	▪ brain

"Oh, no!" cried Zog.

"The computer is broken.

How will we get home now?"

"We must go out onto this planet," Zig said.

"We will find a pine tree."

"But we do not know what it looks like," said Zog.

"We know it is a living thing," said Zig.

"We will use our brains to find it."

He stepped out of the space speeder.

There was green stuff on the ground.

It was soft and cool.

It tickled his feet.

"What is this?" asked Zog.

"I don't know."

Zig bent down.

He pulled some of the green stuff out of the ground.

"It looks like a plant.

But we do not have it on Zorgan."

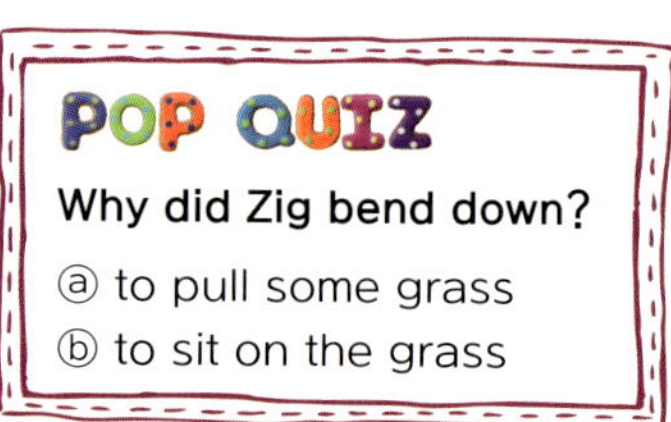

KEY WORDS

- step out of
- tickle
- **bend down** (bend-bent-bent)
- pull

- sniff
- poke out
- tongue
- lick

- chew
- grass
- jump
- scream

He sniffed it.

He poked out his tongue.

He licked the green stuff.

He put some in his mouth.

He chewed it.

"Why are you eating grass?" said a voice.

The voice made Zig jump. Aha!

He turned around.

He screamed.

There stood an alien from Earth. Aha!

It had two eyes instead of three.

It had two arms instead of four.

It had two feet instead of seven.

There was long black hair on its head.

Its skin was brown instead of green.

It looked very strange indeed.

KEY WORDS

- alien
- instead of
- indeed
- shout
- wave
- around
- in circles
- creature
- here

"It is an alien!" shouted Zog.

"Help!"

He waved his arms around.

He ran in circles.

"I am not an alien," said the Earth creature.

"I am a girl."

"A girl?" said Zig.

"What is a girl?"

"I live here," said the girl.

"On Earth.

Where have you come from?"

Zig stepped forward. Aha!

"We are from the planet called Zorgan."

He prodded the girl's arm.

"Are you a living thing?"

She laughed.

"Of course I am."

"How do you know?" asked Zig.

The girl laughed again.

"Because I can see and hear.

I can touch, taste, and smell.

They are called *senses*."

"Can all living things do that?" asked Zig.

"Not all of them," said the girl.

"Animals can, but plants can't.

But they know what is going on around them.

They have different senses."

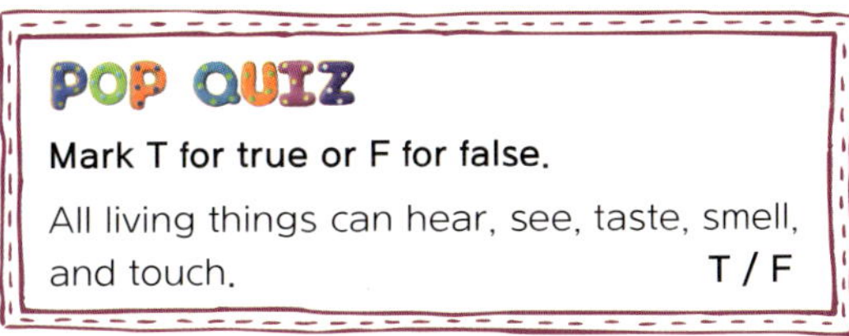

KEY WORDS

- step forward
- be from
- prod
- of course
- because
- sense
- go on
- different

"So how do I know what is living and what is not?" sighed Zig.

"We are looking for a living thing. Will you help us?"

The girl nodded.

"But I must get home in time for supper." 

"What is supper?" asked Zig.

"Is it a living thing?"

"Today, it is chicken and salad."

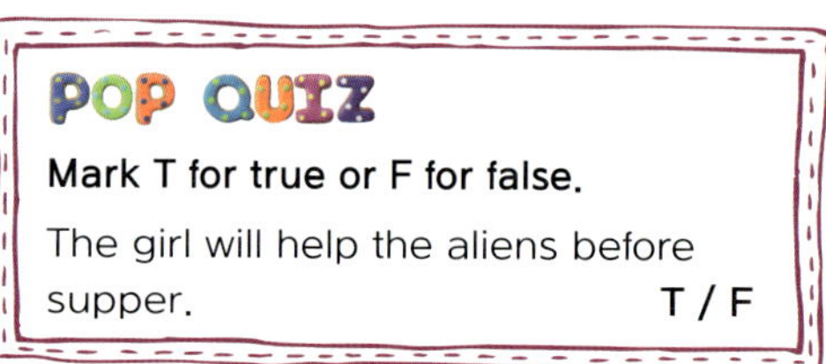

The girl frowned, thinking hard. Aha!

"I suppose it was once alive.

The chicken lived on a farm.

The salad leaves grew in the ground.

All our food comes from animals and plants.

They are living things."

Suddenly, there was a loud shout.

A strange kind of space speeder pulled up.

It had black wheels.

It had red and blue flashing lights on the top.

Some more Earth aliens jumped out of it and ran toward them.

"Here are some more girls," said Zag.

He waved all four of his arms at them.

KEY WORDS

- pull up
- wheel
- flashing
- friendly
- stay
- right

"They are not girls," said the girl.

"They are police officers."

"Are they living things, too?" asked Zig.

"They do not look friendly."

"Stay right there!" shouted one of the police officers.

"Do not move."

He spoke into his radio.

It crackled, and another voice spoke back.

"Is that a living thing?" said Zig.

"No, it's a radio," said the girl.

"He uses it to talk to other people.

It is not a living thing."

"Then why does it speak?" asked Zig.

"A man is speaking through it," said the girl.

"It is a kind of machine.

Machines are not living things.

They are made by people." Aha!

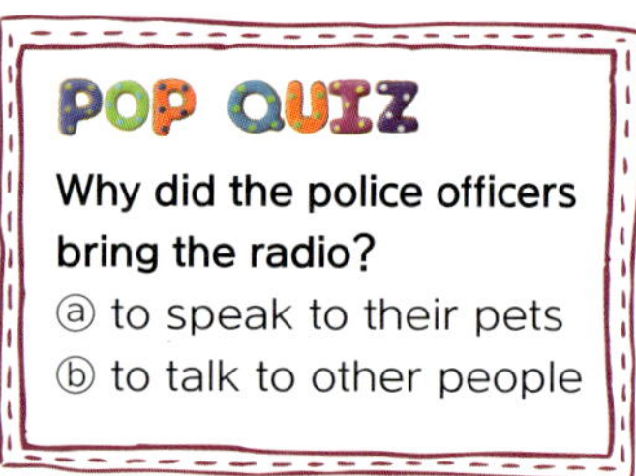

KEY WORDS

- radio
- through
- machine
- be made by

- **understand** (understand-understood-understood)
- even if
- person
- clothes

Zig began to understand.

"So if something is made by a person, it is not a living thing?"

The girl nodded.

"That's right.

A picture is not a living thing even if it is a picture of a person.

Clothes are not living things even if a person wears them."

The police officers were much nearer now.

One of them had a gun.

The girl grabbed hold of Zig's arm.

KEY WORDS

- much
- nearer
- grab hold of

"They want to catch you and lock you up."

"What shall we do?" gasped Zog.

"RUN!" shouted the girl.

- catch
- lock up
- gasp

Comprehension Quiz

A How many eyes, arms, and feet did Zig, Zag, and Zog have?
Circle the correct number for each body part.

❶ eyes   7, 5, 4, 3, 2

❷ arms   7, 5, 4, 3, 2

❸ feet   7, 5, 4, 3, 2

B Choose the correct words that describe the girl.

❶ She had (black / brown) hair.

❷ She had (green / brown) skin.

❸ She had (long / short) hair.

❹ She was from (Zorgan / Earth).

❺ She had (two / four) eyes and arms.

 Choose the best answer to each question.

❶ Why did Zog say the girl was an alien?

a) She was from the planet Zorgan.

b) He had never seen a girl before.

c) She was dressed up as an alien.

d) She had a space speeder.

❷ What do you think the "strange kind of space speeder" really was?

a) a fire engine

b) a rocket ship

c) a police car

d) an ambulance

D Put the sentences in order.

❶ Zig, Zag, and Zog met an alien from Earth.

❷ The girl grabbed hold of Zig's arm and shouted "Run!"

❸ The computer made a fizzing sound.

❹ A strange kind of space speeder pulled up.

❺ Zig, Zag, and Zog stepped out of the space speeder.

________ → ________ → ________ → ________ → ________

A Hiding Game

"We can do better than that," said Zag.

"We can fly."

He grabbed the girl's hand.

He counted.

"Zurble, zorble, zee...!"

Zig, Zag, Zog, and the girl shot up into the air.

"I don't believe it!" shouted the girl.

"I am flying!" Aha!

Below them, the police officers shouted.

They shook their fists.

"Come back here!" they yelled.

KEY WORDS

- do better
- count
- *zurble, zorble, zee*
- air
- fist
- yell

"Where can we find a... a pine tree?" asked Zig.

"There are lots of trees on the hill."

The girl pointed to a low hill.

It was on the other side of the town.

"A tree is a kind of plant, like grass.

But it looks very different."

"Let us go and have a look," said Zog. Aha!

"I want to be home by bedtime."

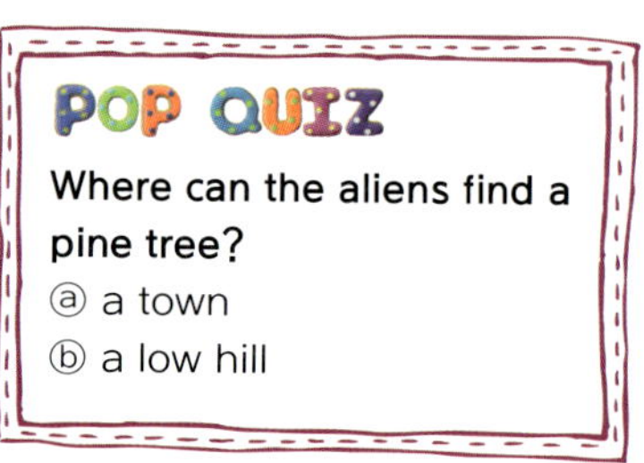

KEY WORDS

- hill
- low
- on the other side of
- let
- have a look
- by

ZOG
ZAG
ZIG

They flew over the town.

They looked down at the buildings.

Cars, buses, and trucks filled the roads.

They honked and hooted.

"Those speeders are making a lot of noise," said
Zig.

KEY WORDS

- fill
- honk
- hoot
- a lot of
- noise
- on one's own
- breathe

"Are they living things?"

"No," said the girl.

"They move, and they make sounds.

But they are not living things."

"Were they made by people?" asked Zog. Aha!

"Yes," said the girl.

"They cannot move on their own.

They do not breathe.

All living things breathe air."

Soon, they arrived at the hill.

They glided down from the sky.

Their feet touched the grass.

Zig pointed at a strange creature walking through the grass.

"What is that?" he said.

"It is a sheep," said the girl.

"It is a living thing.

It grows, and it breathes.

It can make baby sheep.

It can see and hear.

It can smell, touch, and taste.

Those are its senses."

Zig, Zag, and Zog stared at the sheep.

"I do not see the sheep growing," said Zig. **Aha!**

"I do not see the sheep breathing," said Zag.

"I do not see it making baby sheep," said Zog.

POP QUIZ

Choose the right description of the sheep.

ⓐ It has senses.
ⓑ It does not have baby sheep.

The girl laughed.

"It does not grow all the time.

It does not make babies all the time.

But it was much smaller when it was born. **Aha!**

It will have babies in the spring.

It is breathing all the time.

We cannot see it breathing because we are too far away."

"What about the grass?

It does not breathe or have babies," said Zog.

KEY WORDS

- all the time
- be born
- too
- far away
- What about ~?
- take in
- seed
- if
- wet (↔ dry)

"Oh, yes, it does," said the girl.

"It has tiny holes on its leaves.

They take in air.

It makes seeds.

The seeds grow into new grass.

It knows if the day is hot or cold.

It knows if the ground is wet or dry."

"So..." Zig frowned.

"All living things grow.

All living things breathe.

All living things have babies.

All living things have senses. 

They know what is going on around them."

"That's right!"

The girl clapped her hands.

"Now you understand!"

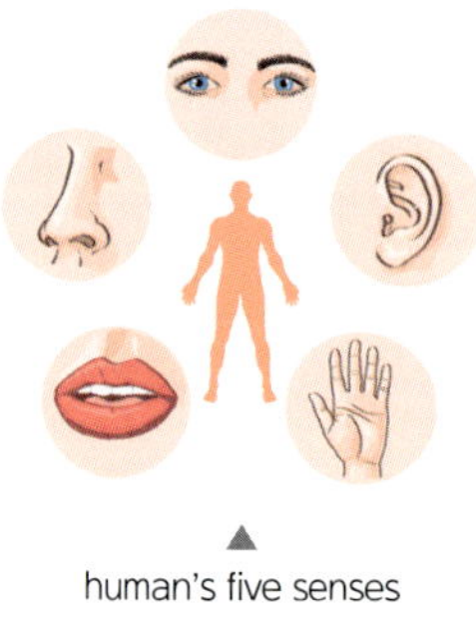

human's five senses

KEY WORDS

- clap hands

ZiG
ZiG
ZiG

Zag climbed onto a large rock.

"Will this rock grow bigger?" he asked.

"On Zorgan, the rocks do not grow.

But Earth rocks might be different."

Zog came over and patted the rock.

He picked up a stone.

"Is this a baby Earth rock?

I think I will keep it as a pet."

KEY WORDS

- climb onto
- might
- come over
- pat
- pick up
- keep

The girl laughed so hard that she fell over. Aha!

She rolled around in the grass.

"The rock does not grow!

It does not make babies!

It is not a living thing.

It has never been alive."

"It is the same as the rocks on Zorgan," said Zig.

He began to laugh, too.

- fall over
- roll around

They walked toward some tall trees on top of the
hill.

A black and yellow striped creature flew by.

It buzzed as it went by.

"That is a bee," said the girl.

"It is a living thing."

Zig heard a strange buzzing sound.

It got louder and louder.

He had to shout over the noise.

"Is that a bee, too?" yelled Zig.

"It is buzzing and flying."

The girl looked up.

"It is a helicopter!" she gasped.

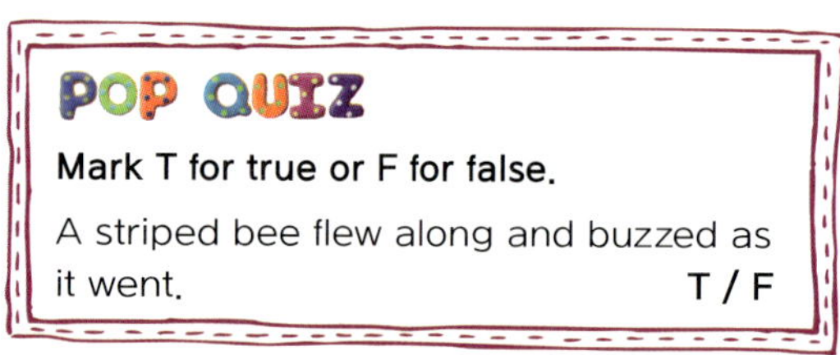

KEY WORDS

- striped
- fly by (fly-flew-flown)
- buzz
- go by

- shout over
- quick
- hide (hide-hid-hidden)
- quickly

- ripple
- enough
- keep up with

"The police officers have found us.

Quick! We must find a place to hide."

Zig, Zag, and Zog began to run.

They ran quickly.

Their seven legs rippled over the grass.

The girl could not run fast enough.

She could not keep up with them.

The helicopter came lower and lower.

Zig, Zag, and Zog ran as fast as they could.

They ran to the top of the hill.

There were lots of trees and bushes there.

Zag and Zog hid in the bushes.

Their skin was green.

The bushes were green.

Nobody could see them.

It was like a hiding game.

"This is called camouflage," said Zag. 

"We are the same color as the bushes.

Nobody can see us."

"But what about me?" cried Zig.

"I am blue.

I cannot hide in the green trees and bushes.

The police officers will see me!"

▲ camouflage

- as ~ as one can
- bush
- hiding game
- camouflage

There were loud shouts behind him.
There was a sound of feet crashing through the trees.
The police officers were coming.

Chapter Three — Comprehension Quiz

A Who said what? Match each line with the right character.

❶    •   • a) "It is the same as the rocks on Zorgan."

❷    •   • b) "Is this a baby Earth rock?"

❸    •   • c) "A tree is a kind of plant, like grass."

❹    •   • d) "This is called camouflage."

B Mark T for true or F for false.

❶ Sheep have baby sheep in the spring.   T F

❷ Some living things don't breathe air.   T F

❸ Grass takes in air through the holes on its leaves.   T F

❹ There is a difference between Earth rocks and Zorgan rocks.   T F

C Choose the best answer to each question.

❶ Why could Zig NOT see the sheep growing?

a) It was not a living thing.

b) He had bad eyesight.

c) It was too far away.

d) It grew very slowly.

❷ Why did Zig think the helicopter was a bee?

a) It stung him.

b) It made a strong wind.

c) It was black and yellow.

d) It made a buzzing sound.

D Put the sentences in order.

❶ Zig, Zag, and Zog arrived at the hill.

❷ Zig understood what living things are.

❸ The police officer had found them with a helicopter.

❹ Zag and Zog hid in the bushes.

❺ Zig saw a strange creature walking through the grass.

_________ → _________ → _________ → _________ → _________

Chapter Four

Sticky Stuff

Zig looked up.

He looked down.

He looked all around.

Where could he hide?

He had a good idea.

He flew up into the air.

He sat at the top of a tall tree.

It was prickly and tickly.

Zig found it hard to sit still and to be quiet. Aha!

POP QUIZ

Why did the police officers not see Zig?

ⓐ He was up in a tree.
ⓑ He had gone down the hill.

KEY WORDS

▪ prickly

▪ tickly

▪ anywhere

Down below,

the police looked all around.

"Where did they go?"

asked one of them.

"I cannot see them anywhere."

The girl was with them.

"I think they went down the hill," she said.

It was not true.

But the police officers listened to her.

They ran down the hill.

Zag and Zog jumped out from the bushes.

Zig flew down from the tree.

"Thank you!" they cried.

"Now, we must find a pine tree."

The girl laughed.

"Look behind you."

Zig, Zag, and Zog turned around.

They looked at the prickly tree.

KEY WORDS

- look behind
- be covered with
- rough
- bark
- explain
- lean against

It was covered with rough brown bark.

"That is a pine tree," said the girl.

"But how will it help you to get home?"

"We need the resin," explained Zag.

"It is like Zorgan fuel.

It will make our space speeder fly again."

Zog leaned against the tree.

"We just want to go home," he said sadly.

Suddenly, he jumped up.

"Ugh! What is this sticky stuff on the tree?

It is all over me. It smells funny."

"That is the resin," said the girl.

"I like the smell.

It is clean and fresh."

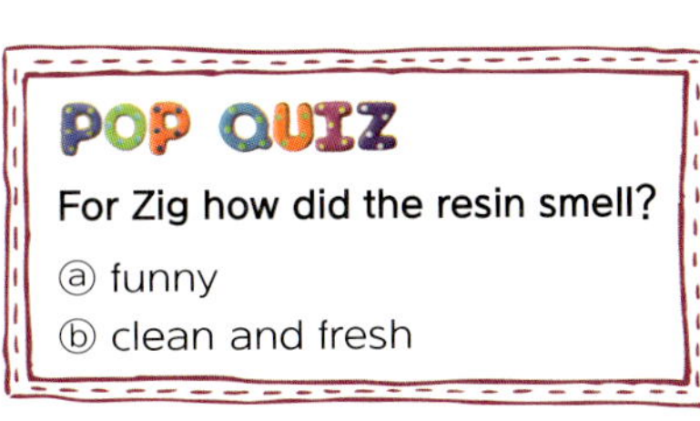

A shout made them jump.

"The aliens must be here somewhere." Aha!

It was the police again.

"We need to collect the resin quickly," said Zag.

"But how?" asked Zog.

"We have nothing to put it in."

"I know!" shouted Zig.

"Let us all lean against the tree trunk, like Zog.

The resin will stick to us.

We can take it back to the space speeder."

Everyone agreed that it was a wonderful idea.

Zig, Zag, and Zog rubbed themselves against the

tree.

KEY WORDS

- somewhere
- collect
- nothing
- trunk

- stick to (stick-stuck-stuck)
- agree
- as … as ~
- glue

- almost
- drop
- pine needle

Soon, they were covered with resin.

It was as sticky as glue.

"Hurry," said the girl.

"The police officers are almost here.

They will see you."

But Zig had another good idea.

He dropped to the ground.

He rolled around in the pine needles.

The needles stuck to the resin.

When Zig stood up, he looked like a pine tree.

Zag and Zog did the same thing.

All three of them stood up.

They looked like a row of trees.

Just in time!

The police officers arrived.

They found the girl standing next to three trees.

"Where did those aliens go?" they asked.

"I cannot see them, can you?" said the girl.

The police had to agree.

They shook their heads and went back to their helicopter.

Zig and Zag held the girl's hands.

They jumped up into the air.

They flew around in a circle.

"Come on, Zog," they called.

"It is time to go home." Aha!

"But I cannot move," said Zog.

"I am stuck to the ground."

He tried to move his feet.

But they were too sticky.

"Wait there," said Zag.

"We will get the space speeder.

Then, we will come and pick you up."

KEY WORDS

- a row of
- just in time
- next to
- shake (shake-shook-shaken)
- Come on!
- wait

Zog shivered.

"Hurry," he said.

"I do not want to wait here on my own."

Zig, Zag, and the girl flew back to the space speeder.

They dropped to the ground nearby.

There was a fence around the space speeder.

The police officers had put it there.

A man stood next to it.

He was guarding it.

"What if he sees us?" whispered Zag. **Aha!**

"I will go and talk to him," said the girl.

"Then, he will not see you.

You can get in your space speeder and go home."

Suddenly, Zig felt sad.

He liked the girl.

He did not want to say goodbye to her.

"Thank you for helping us," he said.

"Please come and visit our planet one day."

The girl laughed and hugged him.

- shiver
- nearby
- fence
- guard
- What if ~?
- whisper
- hug

"You are all sticky," she said.

"Go and put the resin in the fuel tank.

I will talk to the guard."

She went to talk to the guard.

She pointed at the sky.

The guard looked up.

He did not see Zig and Zag.

They crept toward the space speeder.

They scraped all the sticky resin off.

They put it into the fuel tank.

"I hope it works," said Zig.

"We must get Zog from the hill."

They went into the space speeder.

POP QUIZ

Why did the guard not see Zig and Zag getting into the space speeder?

ⓐ He was looking up at the sky.
ⓑ His eyes were closed.

KEY WORDS

- tank
- creep (creep-crept-crept)
- scrape off
- hope
- work
- ready
- happen
- roar

"Ready?" said Zag.

"Ready," said Zig.

Zag pressed the switch.

Nothing happened.

Zag pressed it again.

There was a loud roar, and the space speeder
shook.

The guard turned around.

"Stop!" he yelled.

But the space speeder shot up into the air.

Zig clapped all four of his hands.

"Hooray!" he said.

"Look at your hands," said Zag.

"They are not blue.

They are green again."

Zig began to laugh.

"I think I ate too many blue berries.

I do not need to go to the hospital after all!"

He looked out the round window.

He saw the girl far below.

Zig waved at her until he could not see her any

longer.

Why did Zig not need to go to the hospital?

ⓐ The girl gave him some blue berries.
ⓑ Zig's hands turned green again.

KEY WORDS

▪ hooray
▪ after all
▪ until
▪ any longer

"Goodbye," he whispered.
"Goodbye, my alien friend."

Comprehension Quiz

A Look at the word wall below. Color in the bricks that describe the tree that Zig hid in.

B Put the sentences in order.

❶ The girl went to talk to the guard.

❷ Zig and Zag took off in the space speeder.

❸ Zog was left behind on the hill.

❹ Zig, Zag, and the girl flew back to the space speeder.

________ → ________ → ________ → ________

C

Choose the best answer to the question.

Why did Zog stay behind on the hill?

a) He wanted to be alone.

b) He could not fly.

c) He was stuck to the ground.

d) He wanted to go home a different way.

D

Solve the crossword puzzle with the right word that answers each question.

Across ❷ What did the man next to the fence yell?

❹ Who was standing by the space speeder?

Down ❶ What did Zig say to the girl when he left?

❸ What did Zog tell the others to do when they left him on the hill?

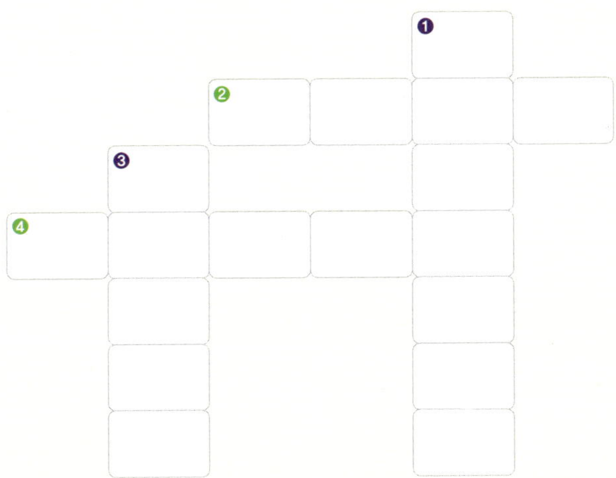

Let's Review the Story

Fill in the blanks to review the story.

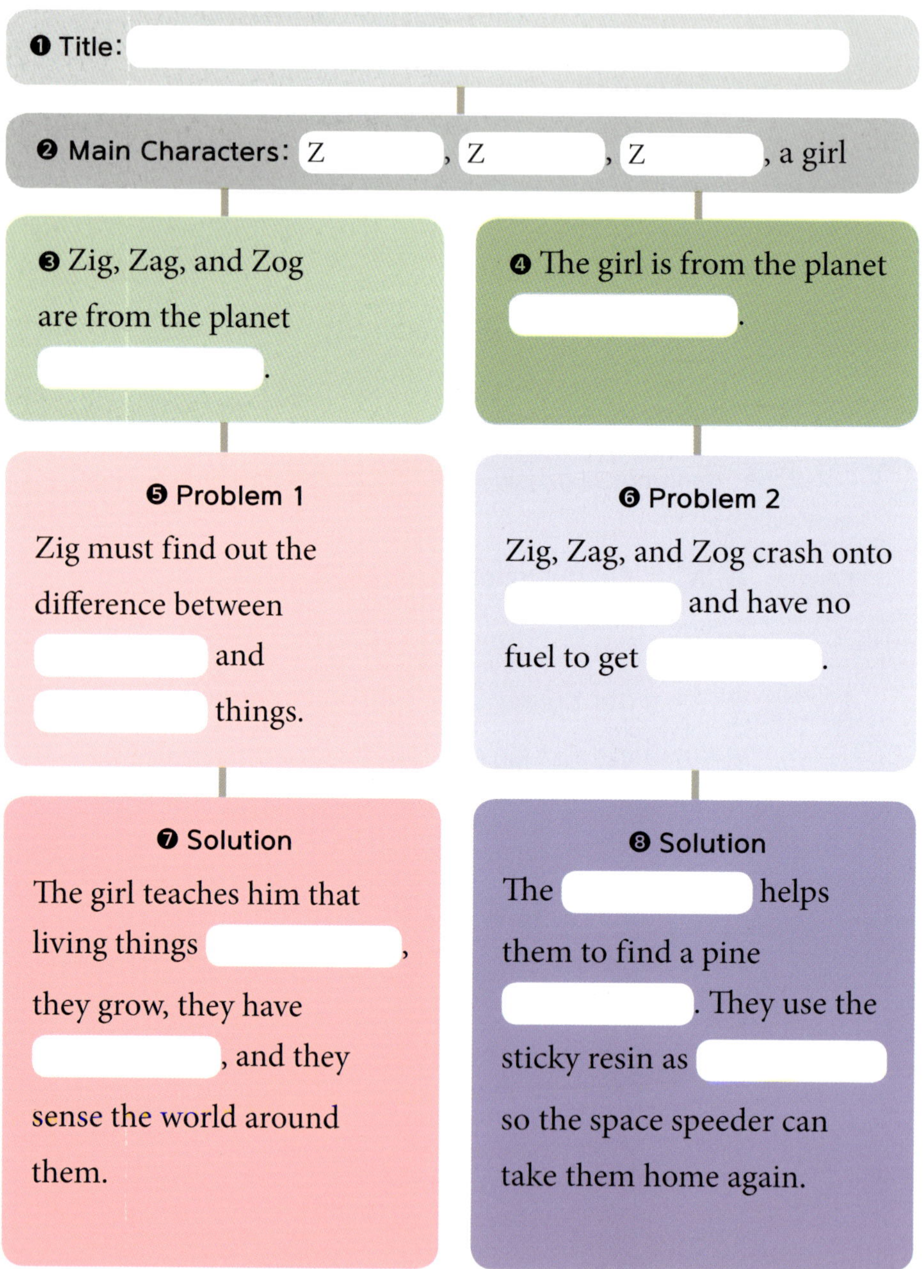

Let's Think & Talk

Let's Think & Talk

Think about the following questions and answer them freely.

❶ Explain the difference between living things and nonliving things.

❷ Do you think aliens really exist in space? Are they our friends or not? Tell us what you think.

❸ Would you help Zig, Zag, and Zog, if you met them as the girl in the story did? Imagine what you would do if you met an alien.

Let's Review the Story

❶ Title: Alien Adventure

❷ Main Characters: Zig , Zag , Zog , a girl

❸ Zig, Zag, and Zog are from the planet Zorgan .

❹ The girl is from the planet Earth .

❺ Problem 1

Zig must find out the difference between living and nonliving things.

❻ Problem 2

Zig, Zag, and Zog crash onto Earth and have no fuel to get home .

❼ Solution

The girl teaches him that living things breathe , they grow, they have babies , and they sense the world around them.

❽ Solution

The girl helps them to find a pine tree . They use the sticky resin as fuel so the space speeder can take them home again.

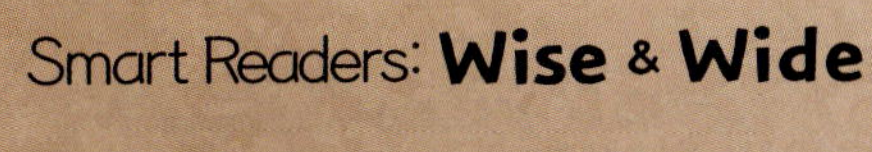

After-reading Test

- Alien Adventure
- Level 2
- 16 Questions

  (Vocabulary 5 / Reading Comprehension 10 /

  Sentence Structure & Grammar 1)

1. Choose all the words which are similar in meaning to the word "tiny".
   ① big
   ② small
   ③ large
   ④ little

2. Which word is NOT related to the same body part?
   ① stared
   ② ran
   ③ jumped
   ④ climbed

3. Which of the following pair has the wrong past tense form of the listed verb?
   ① eat – ate
   ② hurt – hurt
   ③ hide – hide
   ④ bend – bent

4. Which of these words means "agreed"?

   Everyone agreed that it was a wonderful idea.

   ① said
   ② had different thoughts
   ③ thought the same thing
   ④ argued with each other

5. What is the correct word for the blank?

If we run __________ of fuel, the space speeder will crash.

① to   ② in
③ away   ④ out

6. Why did Zig, Zag, and Zog ride in the space speeder?
① to play a game
② to go to school
③ to buy more blue berries
④ to go to the hospital

7. Why did Zag NOT know how to change the direction of the space speeder?
① It was his father's space speeder.
② He could not find the switch.
③ It was a new space speeder.
④ He could not drive any space speeder.

8. What is NOT true about the computer in the space speeder?
① It made a fizzing sound.
② It glowed bright blue.
③ Smoke came out of it.
④ It made a loud bang.

9. When do the sheep make babies?
① winter
② spring
③ summer
④ fall

10. What was NOT mentioned about living things in the story?

    ① It grows.

    ② It breathes.

    ③ It makes fresh air.

    ④ It can see and hear.

11. What is a living thing?

    ① plants

    ② clothes

    ③ machines

    ④ pictures

12. What is NOT a word to describe the smell of resin?

    ① funny

    ② sticky

    ③ clean

    ④ fresh

13. Why did Zog tell Zig and Zag to hurry?

    ① He was cold.

    ② It was getting darker.

    ③ He was very hungry.

    ④ He did not want to be on his own.

14. What did the girl point at so that the guard would NOT look at the aliens?

    ① the fence

    ② the sky

    ③ the stars

    ④ the pine tree

15. Why did Zig's hands turn green again?
    ① He stopped eating blue berries.
    ② The hospital made him better.
    ③ The girl gave him some medicine.
    ④ He wiped them on the grass.

16. What is the wrong part of the sentence?

I have never hear of it.
 ①   ②   ③   ④

Sarah J. Dodd
Sarah J. Dodd is an experienced primary school teacher who resides in the UK, but has also taught in Australia.
She has a PhD in Science and a certificate in Creative Writing. She has published four books for younger children
— 'An Angel Anyway' (Anyway Press) and the Little Angels' series (Lion Hudson plc). Her children's Bible will be
published in 2015. She is currently working on a novel for 9-12 year olds and another for young adults.

Alien Adventure

Written by Sarah J. Dodd
Illustrated by Nika Tchaikovskaya

First Published in December 2014
Second Printing in November 2020

Editors: Kyunghee Jang, Jiyeong Park, Juyon Choi
Designer: Eunhee Lee
Cover Designer: Eunhee Lee

Published and distributed by Happy House, an imprint of DARAKWON
Darakwon Bldg., 211 Moonbal-ro, Paju-si, Gyeonggi-do, Korea 10881
Tel: 82-2-736-2031(ext. 250)   Fax: 82-2-732-2037
Homepage: www.ihappyhouse.co.kr
Publisher: Kyudo Chung

ISBN: 978-89-6653-160-8 18740 / 978-89-6653-156-1 18740(set)

[Components]
• 1 Audio CD (Recording Studio: Aram)
• Answer Keys & Korean Translation: Free download at www.ihappyhouse.co.kr